Sprint

Jonny Zucker

FULL FLIGHT

Titles in Full Flight 3

Web Cam Scam	Jillian Powell
Nervous	Tony Norman
Splitzaroni	Kathryn White
Missed Call	Jillian Powell
Space Pirates	David Orme
Basketball War	Jonny Zucker
Survival	Chris Buckton
Killer Sharks	Stan Cullimore
Sprinters	Jonny Zucker
Dangerous Stunts	Jonny Zucker

Badger Publishing Limited
26 Wedgwood Way, Pin Green Industrial Estate, Stevenage,
Hertfordshire SG1 4QF
Telephone: 01438 356907. Fax: 01438 747015.
www.badger-publishing.co.uk
enquiries@badger-publishing.co.uk

Sprinters   ISBN 1 84424 247 1

Series Editor: Jonny Zucker   Publisher: David Jamieson
Editor: Paul Martin   Design: Jain Birchenough
Cover photo: Linford Christie & Ian Mackie, 25/8/1996 ©
EMPICS
Photos © PA Photos; pp. 1, 4, 8, 11, 29, 31 © EMPICS;
p. 15 © Peter Andrew.

Sprinters

Jonny Zucker

Contents

1. The Fastest People On Earth   4
2. The Sprinters' Kit   6
3. The Race Starts   8
4. Running Style   10
5. Sprint Training   12
6. You Are What You Eat   14
7. The Finish Line   16
8. Who Won?   18
9. The Sprint Relay   20
10. The Paralympics   22
11. Drugs   24
12. Sprint Hurdles   26
13. Record Breakers   28
14. Sprinting Practice   30

Badger Publishing

1. The Fastest People On Earth

- Do you think you can run fast?
- Could you be a record breaker?

People have tried time and time again to prove they are the fastest runners on Earth. In fact, the first recorded Olympic Games took place nearly 3,000 years ago. Today, sprint races are seen by many as the most exciting of all athletics events.

The word 'sprint', means 'a short race at full speed'. The term 'sprint races' means the 100m, 200m and 400m.

Some runners discover that only one of the sprint distances is right for them. Others find they can compete in two sprint races, such as the 200m and 400m. If you want to make it as a sprinter, it's never too early to begin, but to start you'll need the right gear.

2. The Sprinters' Kit

To look the part, you'll need a special thigh-length running suit. These suits hug your body and stop your upper legs getting cold. It's also important for you to choose the right running shoes.

Michael Johnson off to a flying start, showing the right kit.

These have a toe that slopes up and supports your feet. They are light and comfortable.

It was all very different a hundred years ago. In those days, sprinters wore long shorts and long-sleeved shirts. These flapped around on a windy day and slowed the runner down.

Running shoes then were also very different. They were made of leather and had spikes on the bottom to cling to the running track. They were heavy and not very comfortable.

3. The Race Starts

Next time you watch sprinters on TV, watch the start of the race carefully. Sprint races begin with the runners using electronic 'starting blocks'. Each runner can move their blocks so that they are a perfect fit for their own feet.

Michael Johnson on the blocks, showing his running shoes.

The runner puts their feet onto these blocks and crouches down with their fingertips just behind the starting line. The firing of the electronic starting gun marks the start of the race.

Any movement on these electronic blocks can be seen and heard by the race judges. They make sure that none of the runners' feet move before the starting gun. If a runner is judged to have moved off their blocks before the gun sounds, this is called a 'false start'.

If there is a false start, the runners are called back and the race has to start again. Sometimes, sprinters have to put up with several false starts before the race can be run.

4. Running Style

There are some things that all sprinters need to do:

- You must look ahead and not try to see how other runners are doing. This slows you down.
- You need to use your upper arms and shoulders to 'pump' your arms, which helps move your body forward.
- You have to stick to your own lane. If you find yourself in another lane, you will be out of the race.

There are some runners who have their own special running style. The most amazing of these is Michael Johnson, who ran in his famous 'upright' style.

Many running coaches said that
Johnson's style meant he would never
make it as a top sprinter. He wanted to
prove them all wrong and before the
1996 Atlanta Olympics, he said:

I want to give people something to remember.

He did just that, by becoming the first
runner ever to win both the 200m and
400m races.

5. Sprint Training

Sprint training is very hard. On a
normal day, you will start with a
training session in the morning. This
will be the hardest and longest session
of the day. It will include stretching,
weight-training and sprint practice.

Linford Christie oversees a rugby sprint training session.

In the afternoon, you will practise some more sprint exercises, working on your starting and finishing. You may also complete a longer run in the early evening, to improve your fitness level and tone your muscles. Many sprinting coaches were fine runners themselves.

One of the most famous coaches is Britain's Linford Christie. At one time he was the 100m Olympic champion.

Darren Campbell celebrates with coach, Linford Christie.

6. You Are What You Eat

If you want to make it as a top runner, then these foods are off the menu:

- Pizza
- Crisps
- Foods fried in lots of oil, like chips.

You'll need to follow a very special diet.

You have to build up your muscles and avoid putting on fat. Eating well can be the difference between being a good runner and a record breaker.

Your diet will contain plenty of fruit, vegetables, bread and pasta. It is vital that you get the right balance of vitamins and minerals in your body. You'll also need to drink lots of water and special sport drinks.

7. The Finish Line

Sprint races are over so quickly that world-class runners need run at their fastest for less than 10 seconds. How you finish a race is very important. There may only be a tiny gap between the winner of the race and the runner up.

Sprinters are taught to dip their heads at the finish line to push themselves further ahead of the other runners. They are also trained to run 'through' the finish line instead of 'pulling up' before they reach it.

US sprinter Marion Jones wins the 100m.

8. Who Won?

With the help of computers, judges today can tell very quickly who came first in a sprint race. This is very different from how sprint races used to be judged. Before the computer age, a sprint race would have a judge standing at the end of each lane with a timer. They would time the runner in their lane and at the end of the race all of the runner's times would be compared and the winner declared.

At athletics events today, sprinters and the crowd can often see race times on digital boards, split seconds after the race has finished.

Michael Johnson celebrates a new 400m world record, 1999.

At the 1996 Atlanta Olympics, Michael Johnson won the 400m final. The crowd could see his time on a digital score board, as soon as the race was finished. To Johnson's delight, his time of 43.18 seconds was a new world record.

9. The Sprint Relay

For these races, every team has four runners, who will each be running a sprinting distance, for example, 100m. In this case, the race will be called the 4 x 100 sprint relay. These are the steps involved in a sprint relay:

1) The person who is running carries a short piece of metal called a 'baton'.
2) As they get close to the next runner they must hand over the baton without dropping it.
3) Runners hold the baton in their left hand and pass it to the right hand of the runner in front of them.
4) The runner collecting the baton runs off with the baton in their right hand, but switches it to their left hand as they're running, so they can pass it to the next runner's right hand.

5) As the baton is passed the runners need to be running side by side for a few split seconds so that the fastest speed is achieved.

Runners spend hours practising passing the baton, as it is very difficult to get it 100% perfect. However hard a team practises, there are still times when the baton is dropped and the race lost.

10. The Paralympics

The Paralympics are the Olympic Games for disabled athletes and there is huge world interest in these events. As with the Olympics, there is a lot of excitement about the Paralympic sprinting races.

Disabled sprinters finish races in incredible times. The fastest disabled sprinters in the world can complete the 100 metres just 10% slower than able-bodied runners. This is all the more amazing as some disabled sprinters have lost one or both legs and run with replacement legs.

Lukas Christen of Switzerland wins gold in the 200m, ahead of Canada's Earle Connor, Sydney Paralympics 2000.

11. Drugs

Some athletes think that by taking a certain drug, they will improve their sprinting time. This is a bad idea because:

a) Taking drugs can harm an athlete's body.
b) It is against all athletic rules to take any drug that could help you to become faster.

Drug tests are carried out on sprinters in most athletics events. If you win an Olympic sprint medal, you are tested for drugs. If you are found to have taken a drug, then you will face a long ban from sprinting and in some cases you will be banned from ever running again.

The most famous case of a sprinter using drugs took place at the 1988 Olympic Games in Seoul, Korea. Ben Johnson won the 100m in world-record time and was seen by everyone as a truly great sprinting hero. Three days after the race, Johnson was found guilty of taking a drug and was forced to give back his gold medal.

Ben Johnson wins the 100m before failing his drugs test, 1988.

12. Sprint Hurdles

Sprint races are short but very tough. For some runners, sprinting is not enough. There are many athletes who choose to run in 'hurdles' sprint races.

A hurdle is a metal stand with a bar across the top. If you choose to run in a hurdles race, you will have to sprint and jump over a set of hurdles to reach the finish line. Hurdlers have a special running style. They leap over the hurdles with their front leg and bring their other leg over the hurdle behind them.

Timing is everything in a hurdles race. If you don't get your timing right, you may 'clip' the hurdles with your front or your back leg, slowing you down.

In some cases, runners knock a whole hurdle over and fall with it. If this happens, you are out of the race.

One of the finest sprint hurdlers of all time was Welsh athlete Colin Jackson, who picked up many gold, silver and bronze medals in his running career.

Colin Jackson on his way to winning the 60m hurdles, 2002.

13. Record Breakers

All sprinters want to break records. There are two main sprint records - the World record and the Olympic record. Sometimes the Olympic record *is* the World record. The Olympic sprint records have changed a lot over the years. Look at these record breaking facts:

- At the 1896 Olympic Games, the men's record for the 100m was 12 seconds.
- By 1928, it was 10.8 seconds.
- Today it is under 10 seconds.
- Women began taking part in the Olympic Games 100m sprint in 1928, when the record was 12.2 seconds.
- Now there is about a 1 second difference between the men's 100m record and the women's 100m record.

- At the 1984 Sarajevo Olympics in Yugoslavia, American Carl Lewis incredibly won 4 events - the 100m, 200m, sprint relay and long jump.

Lewis described the 1984 Olympics as:

The greatest time of my life.

His record matched that of another American, Jesse Owens in the 1936 Olympics in Berlin, Germany. But Lewis's race times were faster.

14. Sprinting Practice

Here are some tips to improve your sprinting.

1. Practise your starting. Crouch down in the start position and get a friend to say "one, two, three, GO!" As soon as you hear "GO!" push off from the ground with your feet as fast as you can. Practise this again and again until you are pleased with your start.

2. For sprint relay, work with a friend on practising your baton 'change over'. Run 20 metres with a baton (or a ruler if you can't find one) in your left hand and pass it to your friend's right hand.

Remember, for a few seconds as you pass over the baton, you will be running side by side. Your friend will collect the baton in their right hand and switch it to their left hand after a few strides.

If you do want to be a great sprinter, now is the time to start practising. Good luck!

Linford Christie, Barcelona Olympics 100m final, 1992.

Index

athletes 22, 24, 26

athletics 5, 18, 24

baton 20-21, 30-31

Campbell, Darren (13)

Christen, Lukas (23)

Christie, Linford
   (1, 12), 13, (31)

Connor, Earle (23)

coaches 11, 13

diet 14-15

digital boards 18-19

disabled 22

exercises 13

false start 9

finish line 16, 26

finishing 13, 16

hurdles 26-27

Jackson, Colin 27

Johnson, Ben 25

Johnson, Michael
   (6, 8), 10-11, 19

Jones, Marion (17)

judges 9, 18

lane 10, 18

Lewis, Carl 29

medal 24-25, 27

Olympic champion 13

Olympic Games
   5, 11, 22, 25, 28
   Atlanta, 1996 11, 19
   Barcelona, 1992 (31)
   Berlin, 1936 29
   Sarejavo, 1984 29
   Seoul, 1988 25

Owens, Jesse 29

Paralympics 22-23

record 4, 15, 19, 25, 28

relay 20, 30

running shoes 6-7

running style 10, 26

running suit 6

shirts 7

shorts 7

sprint distances 5, 20

sprint races
   5, 8, 16, 18, 22, 26

starting 13, 30

starting blocks 8

starting gun 9

training 12, 16